CLIFF RICHARD

" QUOTE UNQUOTE "

CLIFF RICHARD

" QUOTE UNQUOTE "

Carole Portland

PARRAGON

PICTURE CREDITS

Retna: 74; © King Collection back cover; © Holland 48; © Michael Putland 49, 69, 71; © Kees Tabak front cover, 53; © Adrian Boot 62, 63; © Patrick Quigly 72; Tobi Corney 76; **Ronald Grant Archive**: 6, 22, 25, 27, 28, 30, 33, 34, 35, 40, 43, 45, 55, 56, 58; **Redferns**: 10, 38; © David Redfern 9, 36, 50, 57, 65, 70, 75; © Rick Richards 11, 12, 13; © Gems 14; © Richie Howells 18, 39, 46; T. Hanley 41; Tony Russell 59; © Mick Hutson 60; © Overseas 66; © Erica Echenburg 79

First published in Great Britain in 1996 by
Parragon Book Service Ltd
Unit 13–17
Avonbridge Trading Estate
Atlantic Road
Avonmouth
Bristol BS11 9QD

ISBN: 0-7525-1696-5

Produced by Haldane Mason, London

Art Direction: Ron Samuels
Editor: Charles Dixon-Spain
Design: Errol Campbell
Picture Research: Charles Dixon-Spain

Printed in Italy

CONTENTS

BAD BOY ROCKER

'I believe I'm the only real rocker, because I'm the only one who really concentrates on what I'm doing. All that other stuff has nothing to do with rock'n'roll, it's to do with being children and never growing up. If the people that smash hotel rooms weren't in rock'n'roll they'd probably be in a remand home.'

FACING PAGE: 'I never wanted to be a singer until I heard Elvis . . .'

Harry Webb was a chubby-cheeked Teddy Boy when he was spotted by Bob Greatorex at a basement coffee house called the 2i's in London's Soho district. His band didn't have a bass player and his only recording was a £10 demo from the HMV Records shop in nearby Oxford Street. He was just a teenage kid with a dream of stardom. But that night in the 2i's when Harry Webb changed his name he set in motion a career which has spanned five decades, more than 100 singles and 59 albums. That night, the Cliff Richard legend began.

Rodger and Dorothy Webb were truly children of the British Empire – he had been born in Burma just after the First World War, she in India at the height of the British Raj, and neither had ever been to Britain. Similarly their son and first child Harry Rodger was born in Lucknow, India on October 14, 1940, to be followed by two daughters, Donella and Jacqueline. Despite the inroads Germany and its allies were making in Europe, Africa and the Far East, it seems the Webbs were a comfortable and prosperous family, living quite happily from Rodger's earnings as a manager in a firm of caterers.

The idyllic life the family had made for themselves in India was to be shattered soon after the end of the Second World War, however. In 1947 India gained independence from the British. This alone would not have forced the Webbs out, but the Viceroy caused great political upheaval by dividing the subcontinent along religious lines. India became a place of bloodshed and hardship and the Webbs were forced to make the decision to leave. At first they thought of going to Australia, but Dorothy found the idea of 'returning' to her homeland much more appealing. Consequently, with Harry less than eight years old, the Webbs booked passage on the wartime troopship SS *Ranchi* and arrived in Britain three weeks after embarkation. Having no money and no other place to go the family relied on the charity of Dorothy's mother, whoat least could provide a roof over their heads. For a while 14 members of the family lived in a house with only three bedrooms.

Eventually Rodger found a job as a clerk at the Atlas Lamps factory in Enfield, Middlesex, and the family – along with the newly born third daughter, Joan – moved into a council house in Hargreaves Close, Cheshunt,

Hertfordshire. It was a far cry from the days of the Raj when the Webbs were waited on by four Indian servants. Rodger had to cycle 11 km (7 miles) to work and, after spending the day taking care of her four children, Dorothy went to work in the evenings at a paint brush factory. At school, Harry proved to be more physical than academic, excelling in drama and a number of sports including football and athletics. He failed his Eleven Plus exam and finally left school with only one 'O' level, in English.

Thanks to his father, Harry was offered a job at Atlas Lamps for £4.15s a week. So like his father he began to

'When I was at school I had lots of pals . . . My house is still there and any of my old mates are welcome to come any time and my mother takes care of us all. But it isn't like that any more. Suddenly these old friends, my one-time gang, are all peculiar and stiff and strange.'

Sincerely
Cliff Richard

make the arduous cycle ride to Enfield,
but unlike his father he dreamt of something much more exciting: Harry Webb
planned on becoming a rock'n'roll star.

Music had captured his imagination at
an early age. At school he had been part
of a vocal group called the Quintones,
performing at local dances, but the five
singers had split up when the three
female members all left for secretarial
college. Harry's future only began to
take shape when his father gave him his
first guitar and he discovered rock'n'roll.

In 1955 Bill Haley & The Comets
scored a huge Number One hit with
the single 'Rock Around The Clock',
introducing a new kind of music to the
British public and more particularly the
young Harry Webb. Rock'n'roll, Bill
Haley-style, seemed exciting and new,
although in truth it was merely a
watered-down version of American 'race
music', or Rhythm and Blues, which had
been around for many years. Haley and
his band were wild and wacky on stage,

*'People don't believe it, but I used to swear
like a trooper.'*

playing a type of music which hinted at
mischief and sexuality never heard on the
radio before. When the group came to
England Harry played truant from school
to travel to Kilburn in London and line
up for tickets to the concert. The effect
on him was electric.

Meanwhile, the skiffle craze was
sweeping the nation thanks to Lonnie
Donegan's 1956 runaway hit single 'Rock
Island Line', inspiring thousands of young
people around Britain to form ad hoc
groups. To a skiffle band a washboard
and a few tin pots were percussion
instruments and a broomstick wedged

ABOVE: With Ian
Samwell, backstage at
an Everly Brothers' show
in 1959.

into an old tea chest was a primitive single-string bass. Add to those a cheap guitar and three chords and you had yourself a rock'n'roll band of sorts. Donegan was closely followed by Elvis Presley and it wasn't very long before Britain was creating its own rock'n'roll idols, most notably the salt-of-the-earth

'I like a lot of the underground bands but I can't understand why they feel they have to appear on stage looking like a bunch of tramps. When people pay good money they expect everything to be right, including a well-turned-out appearance. I wouldn't feel my best unless I went on stage looking smart.'

Cockney Tommy Steele. Not to be out-done, Harry Webb decided to audition for a local band called the Dick Teague Skiffle Group, which was in need of a singer. He was accepted but, like Teague's drummer Terry Smart, Harry

yearned for something bigger and better. So, with his old school friend Norman Mitham, he formed a trio called Harry Webb and the Drifters.

The group played at local dances and youth clubs until, in 1957, they were spotted in the Five Horseshoes pub in Hoddeston, Hertfordshire by an 18-year-old Teddy Boy named John Foster. Although he worked at the local sewage works and knew nothing whatsoever about the music business, Foster fancied that he had discovered a star of the future and with no further ado offered to be the group's manager. Flattered that

ABOVE: Norrie Paramor (right) signed Cliff to EMI in 1958. Carol Costa (centre right) was to become Jet's wife and Cliff's one and only lover.

anyone should take an interest in them, the group naively agreed.

It could have been the worst decision they ever made, but fortunately Foster assumed the role of manager with complete conviction. He persuaded his mum to finance the group's first-ever recording. In the HMV store in Oxford Street they recorded versions of 'Lawdy Miss Clawdy' and 'Breathless' for the princely sum of £10. Armed with the demo, John Foster began the difficult task of persuading record companies, agents and promoters to listen to the Drifters in action. His first success was a visit to the famous 2i's coffee bar in London's Soho district where the proprietor, Paul Lincoln, had a reputation for giving an early break to up-and-coming performers, including Tommy Steele himself. Lincoln agreed to book the group and the boys arrived in London for their first show fully expecting to be 'discovered' and showered with fame and fortune. It didn't happen.

Fame would come later, but – although they did not know it at the time – Fortune was smiling on Harry Webb, Terry Smart and Norman Mitham. One night at the 2i's, they were approached by a red-haired young RAF serviceman who suggested that what the Drifters

LEFT: Cliff in the recording session which resulted in his first hit single, 'Move It'. As Cliff said later, the single 'has to be the first-ever rock'n'roll record made in Europe'.

really needed was a lead guitarist (even though both Harry and Norman were guitarists and the Drifters needed a bass player desperately!). Volunteering his services, Ian Samwell was accepted on the spot. During their second week at the 2i's the band was spotted by Bob Greatorex, a well-known promoter and talent scout. Greatorex took the group out for a drink at a nearby pub and, out of the blue, invited them to perform at a

The Ripley show was a turning point for the group. That night they barely earned enough money to cover their travel expenses and were forced to sleep

---

'I actually used to be a bit fat. I'd never even thought about it till one evening I was sitting watching CORONATION STREET on telly; Ena Sharples made a remark about "that chubby Cliff Richard" — I was horrified!'

---

one-off dance hall show in Ripley, Derbyshire. He had one condition, however; Harry Webb's name should be changed because it sounded too ordinary. After much discussion they all agreed on the name Cliff, but the surname was not so easy. They thought about Cliff Russard and then Cliff Richards. Then Ian Samwell suggested that the 's' should be dropped, the idea being that when Harry corrected people who got it wrong they would be more likely to remember the name. Although he was still living in a tiny council house, Harry Webb took the first steps towards fame in the time it took to drink a pint of beer.

on benches at the dance hall because they were too late to get the last train home. But these things didn't matter. When Cliff stepped out on to a real stage for the first time — dressed as a Teddy Boy in a bright pink jacket, matching pink socks, black drainpipe pants and black shirt — the incredible roar of the crowd made him feel like a star. From then on, he would let nothing stand in his way.

That summer Cliff Richard and the Drifters made an appearance at the Gaumont Theatre in Shepherd's Bush, London, during a Saturday matinee

RIGHT: *One of Cliff's first appearances on* Oh Boy! *The producer of the show, Jack Good, said later, '[Cliff] was about four inches shorter than he is now.'*

variety show for teenagers. The London audience gave them the same riotous welcome they had received in Ripley. 'We just weren't used to that sort of reaction from people,' recalls Norman Mitham, 'It was the first reaction we ever had to Cliff as a sex symbol. In Soho and Ripley you thought they were getting excited at the music but in Shepherd's Bush the audience was seated and they were screaming at Cliff.' On June 14, 1958 the group appeared as special guests at the same venue and the screams were so loud that Cliff could barely hear himself sing, let alone follow what the Drifters were playing.

Watching from the crowd of scream-ing teenagers was a London booking agent called George Ganjou, a former cabaret artiste from Poland who knew nothing about rock'n'roll music. John Foster had picked his name out of a list of agents in the telephone book and used his gift of the gab to tempt him to Shepherd's Bush. The show reinforced George Ganjou's opinion that rock'n'roll was a silly teenage craze which would never last, but he also saw in Cliff Richard an opportunity to make a lot of money. 'As soon as Cliff started to sing,' Ganjou recalled, 'they all – especially the

girls – went mad. They started to shout and rush towards him, and after seeing this I decided I'd better go backstage and have a talk to him.' Ganjou was in his fifties, with a lifetime's experience as an entertainer and was also sole booking agent for Butlin's. 'He was not a Caruso,' admitted Ganjou, 'but as far as crooning was concerned, he had some-thing which appealed to girls and women. Vocal and visual – that's what he was. I knew then that he would become a star, although he was dressed a bit peculiarly.'

The agent agreed to pass the group's demo disc on to his friend Norrie

ABOVE: Although they broke new ground in the music industry, Cliff and the Shadows were entertainers first and foremost.

Paramor, the artiste and repertoire manager at Columbia Records. Like George Ganjou, Paramor was no rock'n'roll fan, but he knew a good thing when it was offered to him. He took the demo disc home and gave it to his teenage daughter, Caroline, who proved his instincts right. 'She flipped when she heard it,' he commented later, 'and she double-flipped when I showed her Cliff's photo.' However, Paramor decided to think about it for a couple of weeks while he went on holiday with his family in Tangier. When Paramor returned to England, it was with relief he heard the news that Cliff Richard was Columbia's latest recording star.

On July 24, 1958, Cliff went to EMI's Abbey Road studio to record two songs. Norrie Paramor produced the session and would remain as Cliff's producer until 1972. 'Schoolboy Crush' was a teenage ballad which had been a hit in America for Bobby Helms. Back in the Fifties pop-singers were never given the luxury of selecting their own material and were certainly not expected to write songs. Cliff had never heard 'Schoolboy Crush' until he was invited to the session with Norrie Paramor, but he was allowed to choose the less important B-side.

Ian Samwell wrote 'Move It' while sitting on the top deck of the bus from Cheshunt to London. He wanted to write an American-sounding record and he hit the bullseye on his first shot. With a twang of Country and the full vocabulary of rock'n'roll (words like 'baby' and

---

'I never wanted to do anything but have hits. I'm unashamedly a hit-maker.'

RIGHT: Cliff with Bruce Welch, who said of their early gigs, 'Often we could not hear ourselves play on stage because we were deafened by the shrill, high-pitched screaming from the fans.'

RIGHT: 'Cliff was very proud of us, particularly Hank.' — Bruce Welch (left)

'groove' did not come naturally from the mouth of a boy from the Home Counties), it was the first true rock'n'roll song to be recorded by an English band. It was also notable for its 'message', promising that rock'n'roll music was not the short-lived craze which 'squares' and grown-ups claimed it to be: 'They say it's gonna die: Oh honey, please, let's face it / They just don't know what's a-goin' to replace it.'

The Drifters were not contracted to Columbia Records, nor were their services required at the recording. In those days singers never shared the spotlight; the musicians were relegated to the background. The best way for an instrumentalist to make a living wage was to be a 'session' musician, either in a studio or at a theatre. Consequently, although Terry Smart and Ian Samwell took part in the recording of the two songs, they were mostly replaced by the far more experienced professionals.

The release date of 'Schoolboy Crush' was set for August, so Ganjou and Paramor set about promoting their fledgling talent. George Ganjou immediately booked the group for nine weeks at a Butlin's camp. Norrie Paramor's connections at the *Daily Mirror* paid off when

Cliff was hailed as a 'New Recruit For The Disc War'. Meanwhile, Franklyn Boyd, the publisher of 'Schoolboy Crush', was also fighting in Cliff's corner to make the song into a chart success. It was Franklyn Boyd who pulled off the biggest success of Cliff's early career, giving the climbing star his first foothold in the world of television.

Boyd launched Cliff into the big time when he approached TV producer Jack Good, a man whose creativity and flair paved the way for young people's entertainment on British TV for years to come. Good, a bespectacled 27-year-old Oxford graduate, was an unlikely-looking rock'n'roll pioneer, but in 1957 he had devised the BBC's first ever rock'n' roll music programme, *6.5 Special*, which had become an unprecedented hit. 'I had always hated pop music,' claims Jack Good now, 'and therefore this rock'n'roll appealed to me in a perverse way because I immediately realized Frank Sinatra would hate it, and I loathed Frank Sinatra.'

In the intervening year Good had fallen out with the BBC, who wanted to tone down his ideas and turn *6.5 Special* into a teenage magazine programme. Instead Good went to the independent television station ATV with a vision of a fast-moving music programme called *Oh Boy!* In many ways it was the precursor to today's fast-moving MTV-style music programming. 'I wanted to create tremendous tension and excitement which I justified in my mind as a kind of catharsis as described by the Greeks,' he

---

'My ultimate ambition is to make a Western with Elvis.'

---

explains. 'I thought that the kids would let off steam in the theatre and would then be passive when they went back on the streets. Absolute rubbish! It worked quite the other way. I should never have been let loose!'

Jack Good listened to 'Schoolboy Crush' and was indifferent. But then he turned the record over to listen to the flip-side, and could not believe what he was hearing. As he wrote in his regular column in *Disc* magazine, 'Move It' woke him up like a slap in the face: 'Wham! This disc could sell 50,000 on its first eight bars alone,' he predicted. 'It kicks off with a forceful, dramatic guitar phrase

that runs an electric shock down the spine. In comes the drum, driving a vicious beat right through the heart of the number.' On the subject of the singer, he continued effusively: 'The diction is clear, the phrasing authentic, professional – there is a real feeling for this Country & Western style. If this disc had been a product of Sun Records of Memphis, Tennessee – the original recording company of Elvis Presley and Jerry Lee Lewis – I should not have been surprised . . . but when one considers that this is the product of a 17-year-old boy from Cheshunt, Hertfordshire, the mind just boggles.' Like Jack Good, the rest of the nation's music press and radio presenters dismissed the saccharine 'Schoolboy Crush' and flipped the record over, effectively making 'Move It' the single's A-side by popular demand.

At the time, Cliff and the Drifters were working at Butlin's in Clacton. Ian Samwell had switched to bass guitar part-time and Cliff's old friend Norman Mitham had been unceremoniously sacked, making the Drifters temporarily a trio once more. Mitham was understandably slighted, but Cliff was convinced that the surplus guitarist was holding them back and he would let nothing –

even friendship – stand in the way of his career. Terry Smart remained on drums and Cliff attempted to play guitar but, in truth, he was never a great musician and was helped out during the group's residency by a Butlin's session man. Along with 'Move It', their set list consisted mainly of Cliff's favourite American hits: Eddie Cochran's 'Twenty Flight Rock', Elvis Presley's 'Heartbreak Hotel' and 'Hound Dog', and the Jerry Lee Lewis classic 'Whole Lotta Shakin' Goin' On'.

They were at work in Clacton when they heard the news that Jack Good wanted Cliff Richard and the Drifters to appear on the first series of *Oh Boy!* For the first show artists were booked for a full week of rehearsals, during which time Jack Good completely transformed Cliff from Teddy Boy to pop idol. Cliff was bewildered and overwhelmed by the television crew and allowed Good to dictate his every movement. Jack Good ordered him to cut off his thick sideburns and worked with him tirelessly to help him perfect his stage persona. 'What you must remember', notes Good, 'is that compared with Tommy Steele and Marty Wilde, who had already been going around the theatres topping the bill, Cliff was raw and although he threw himself into his songs with conviction, he did not project a personality.'

Jack Good decided to portray Cliff Richard as a smouldering teenager, far more innocent than the tough-talking, hip-swinging Elvis Presley but still burning with a latent sensuality, implied by the provocative curl of his upper lip. All that remained of Harry Webb from Middlesex was the shocking pink stage costume which would be his

---

'My voice was hardly broken then. That was my Elvis period, pompadour hair-style, all that. I was the rage of my school because I looked like Elvis: I even used to practise curling my lip the way he did.'

---

trademark for years to come. His debut on *Oh Boy!* was not quite the birth of a pop sensation, but it was certainly a success. 'Move It' began to climb the charts and Cliff Richard sustained the same smouldering persona throughout the first phase of his career.

Meanwhile, more practical matters needed to be attended to. The group was

RIGHT: 'Sometimes I think my mother will wake me up one morning and I'll find myself back to being just plain Harry Rodger Webb, an ordinary clerk.'

booked on its first national tour as support for the visiting American duo the Kalin Twins, but they still had no steady guitarist. So John Foster returned once more to the 2i's in Soho to find a likely candidate. He had arranged a meeting with Tony Sheridan (who went on to work with the Beatles during their time in Hamburg in 1963) but instead met a young Geordie guitarist called Hank B. Marvin. Foster was highly impressed when he heard Marvin play and when he found out that the guitarist was already booked to appear on the Kalin Twins' tour (backing the Most Brothers), he asked him immediately if he would join the Drifters. There was one condition, however: Hank Marvin would not join without his friend and fellow-guitarist Bruce Welch.

There were more changes to come before the year was out. To begin with John Foster was usurped by Franklyn Boyd and demoted from the position of business manager to become Cliff's road manager. Because Foster was still Cliff's friend he was happy to stay on, but it would not be for long. 'I was beginning to learn the business, but I was beginning to learn my limitations as well,' Foster later admitted. 'I was naive

and so was Cliff. We never had a contract between us and we took each other totally on trust. It was a big mistake I suppose. However, I'd gone as far as I could as Cliff's manager.'

Ian Samwell was also on the way out. With 'Move It' riding high in the chart (it eventually peaked at Number Two) and Cliff becoming the regular star of *Oh Boy!*, Samwell was expected to come up with another hit single. The result was 'High Class Baby'. This song was lukewarm compared to its electrifying predecessor and Cliff was bitterly disappointed. He hated 'High Class Baby' and was deeply concerned that it would end his career just as he was getting started. At the same time, the guitar skills of Marvin and Welch were making Samwell's performance look utterly amateurish. After the tour John Foster was given the unenviable task of notifying Ian 'Sammy' Samwell that he had been replaced.

The tour began at the Victoria Hall, Hanley, Stoke on Trent, where the new line-up of the Drifters (Samwell, Smart, Marvin and Welch) performed in public for the first time. The group still lacked a bassist and so Jet Harris, who was playing with the Most Brothers, stepped in from time to time. Jet looked older than the other Drifters, a jazz-lover with bleached blond hair and a reputation for unpredictability who was playing a bass guitar in the days when stand-up double bass was the convention. 'He'd been around a lot longer than we had,' says Hank Marvin, who held him slightly in awe. '[Jet] had a concept of advanced chord sequences and how to play against them. To us he was like the old man of music.' 'He looked incredible,' adds Cliff. 'He had a quiff, he was gaunt . . . he was everything I wasn't. Jack Good once . . . said that only Cliff Richard could ever stand in front of him.' By the end of a tour which had escalated in popularity Jet Harris had become a member of the Drifters. When Cliff's eighteenth birthday came around on October 14, 1958, 2,500 fans sang 'Happy Birthday' to him at the DeMontfort Hall in Leicester and threw presents onto the stage. Cliff was exactly where he wanted to be, basking in the glory, but he was soon to discover that it required a lot of very hard work to keep up the momentum.

Franklyn Boyd was determined not to let his star's popularity slip. Cliff was quickly becoming a seasoned professional in front of the TV cameras, and had even won a part in a new film, but he was still very inexperienced on stage. So Boyd decided that he would put him through a crash course by booking three weeks of London variety shows during which Cliff and the Drifters topped the bill twice nightly alongside comedians and speciality acts. It was an absurd compilation

RIGHT: Serious Charge (1959) featured the songs 'Living Doll', 'No Turning Back' and 'Mad About You', plus the Drifters' song 'Chinchilla'.

'Without the public there would be no Cliff Richard success story. I shall never forget what they've done for me.'
CLIFF PAYS TRIBUTE TO HIS FANS IN THE NME, SEPTEMBER 1959.

---

of artists who were poles apart in the entertainment business, but Boyd was convinced that Cliff should learn his stage-craft the hard way. 'The kids liked him, but he didn't have an act,' he remembers. 'He didn't know how to come on and off stage. He didn't know how to take a bow.'

However, one move which Cliff had perfected was the wiggle of the hip. His appearances on *Oh Boy!* had prepared the (predominantly female) masses for Cliff's

act and the reaction was always the same — deafening, high-pitched, ecstatic screams.

The fact that the rather weak 'High Class Baby' reached Number Seven in the chart was an indication that Cliff Richard could do little wrong. He had quickly deposed Tommy Steele as Britain's top rock'n'roller and his (largely fictional) rivalry with singer and *Oh Boy!* star Marty Wilde had literally made front-page news.

Unfortunately Cliff was too young and inexperienced to handle his fame at first. A fragile boy who was often seen to break down in tears when the stress got too much, Cliff could not cope with the constant and unremitting pressure. He was besieged by ardent fans wherever he turned and he seemed to be working all day and all night. At the end of the most incredibly successful year of his life Cliff ran back to his mother and father in desperation, laying the blame firmly at the feet of Franklyn Boyd. He told his mother, 'I can't stand this life in show-business any longer. If it's all going to be like this last week, I'd rather go back to my old job at Atlas Lamps.'

Although Cliff soon bounced back, the seeds of doubt had already been

> *'I used to go out of the way to make the kids scream. Now they scream when they hear my name.'*

planted in the minds of his parents and they began to follow his affairs far more closely. Because Cliff was under the age of 21 he was legally bound by the decisions of his parents. Rodger Webb decided immediately to notify Franklyn Boyd that his services were no longer required. He then offered the position to Tito Burns, who was agent to the *Oh Boy!* regular Cherry Wainer. Burns was a flashy character with slicked-back hair, a big moustache and a fixed grin. He was a popular band leader as well as a manager and seemed to know everyone in the heady world of West End showbiz — Rodger Webb was bowled over by the impresario's charisma the way young girls swooned over Cliff. Meanwhile, George Ganjou — who was still receiving his regular ten per cent of Cliff's earnings — had faded into the background.

The most shocking change of all was in the new year when John Foster was

NO TURNING BACK

Words and Music by LIONEL BART

FEATURED IN THE FILM

SERIOUS CHARGE

A MICKEY DELAMAR PRODUCTION
DIRECTED by TERENCE YOUNG
DISTRIBUTED by EROS FILMS LTD

LEFT: The director of Serious Charge, Terence Young, went on to make the classic James Bond movies Dr. No, From Russia With Love *and* Thunderball.

given the sack. Rodger blamed him for not 'looking after' his son and there was no further discussion. Despite everything Foster had done for Cliff their friendship was over. In later life Foster became the director of his own public relations company, putting his legendary gift for the gab to great use. Around the same time, Terry Smart made his exit, the last of the original Drifters. Aware that he was out-classed by the newcomers in the band he decided to pursue a career in the merchant navy. Smart was replaced by the 15-year-old drummer Tony Meehan, who was already a professional and had already played with Marvin and Harris.

The year of 1959 began with the release of Cliff's third single, 'Living Doll', which only reached Number 20 in the chart. But while Cliff may have been disappointed, his bank balance was looking very healthy. Overnight he had become one of the nation's biggest-earning entertainers, raking in a massive £15,000 for a 30-week contract with the Grade Agency for concert appearances. Tito Burns once claimed that he was receiving 15 calls an hour from agents, promoters and TV producers who all wanted a piece of Cliff's success.

In April he released his debut album, *Cliff*, recorded at the Abbey Road studio in just two days in front of a small, hand-picked audience. Featuring some of Cliff's favourite hits (Buddy Holly's 'That'll Be The Day', Gene Vincent's

'Someone recently called me a musical parasite, but that's ridiculous. How can I be a parasite when me and the Shads started it all? What the devil do I sing if I don't sing rock'n'roll?'

'Sleep well? No, I haven't slept well for years. Sometimes I wake up four or five times on the hour. Ideally I like eight hours, normally I get perhaps six.'

'Be-Bop-A-Lula' and so on) it reached Number Four in the charts and was boosted by a new single, 'Mean Streak', which reached Number Ten (the flip-side, 'Never Mind', also charted, peaking at Number 21). This marked the end of Cliff's period as a rock'n'roller. Like all the other music business professionals who had advised Cliff Richard on his career to date, Tito Burns did not much care for rock'n'roll music. Burns was convinced that it was on the way out and he did not want to see the boy's stardom end when the fashion faded away. When Cliff's next single came along it seemed like Burns's predictions had been right. Maybe the craze *had* ended.

FAME & FORTUNE

'I used to moan about being recognized all the time and things like that, but that was just immaturity. The one thing that I really wanted was the fame, and I've got it.'

Cliff Richard's success has always been built on music, but his youthful image is forever cemented in the nation's consciousness thanks to his happy-go-lucky musical films. Films like *The Young Ones* and *Summer Holiday* captured all the joy and innocence of youth with timeless stories which appeal to every generation.

Cliff's first acting role was in *Serious Charge*, based on the daring Fifties play of the same title, written by Philip King. The film starred Anthony Quayle as a vicar who tries to help a juvenile delinquent but then finds himself falsely accused of indecently assaulting the boy. Cliff's role was added to provide some light relief from the sordid plot. He played the delinquent's younger brother, Curly Thompson. 'The people who made the film must have been daft,' Cliff laughs. 'I was cast as Curly, but instead of simply changing the name of the character, they went through the painful and complicated procedure of curling my hair with hot tongs every morning before the day's shooting.'

Cliff's role was fairly superficial but he was cast for a very important reason: to sing. Curly Thompson had been given three songs and one of them became Cliff's biggest hit to date, 'Living Doll'. The song was written by Lionel Bart and Cliff hated it at first. It was a quick-tempo tongue-twister which never sounded quite right until Bruce Welch tried slowing it down and giving it a Country and Western 'bass-strum, bass-strum' beat. From that moment on the song had 'hit' written all over it.

'Living Doll' put Cliff's chart career back to full speed. It became his first Number One hit single, his first gold disc and eventually sold almost two million copies. It was Cliff's biggest break in the world of entertainment. Beginning with 'Living Doll', he had a run of 20 hit singles which all sold in excess of a million copies worldwide. He suddenly realized that there was more for him to achieve than the screams of a few thousand adoring teenage girls. With a

'I know you can't please everyone. Even if you sell a million records — and I've done that several times — there are still fifty million people out there who didn't buy it!'

FACING PAGE: 'When I was 14 I used to think how marvellous it would be to be 20 and shave every day.'

> 'Girls are all very well but date them once and then run. Date them twice and they get serious . . . Next thing you know, you're hooked and wondering what's hit you.'
> CLIFF IN SUMMER HOLIDAY

ABOVE: The Shadows line-up changed many times, with Hank Marvin (right) and Bruce Welch (left) as the mainstays. Both were in Summer Holiday. John Rostill (centre left) and Brian Bennett (centre) joined later.

song like 'Living Doll' he could touch the hearts of men, women and children of all ages. Moreover, if he was going to survive as a performer, he would have to strive to appeal to all of the people all of the time, no matter how fashion changed. That realization helped Cliff through the next 35 years of his career and beyond, always singing what the people wanted to hear. 'What we were discovering was that rock'n'roll seemed to be fairly limited', he remembers, 'because the public weren't buying it in hundreds of thousands. We were the first rock teenagers and ten-year-olds had no money to spend, so in the end records like 'Living Doll' sold because they appealed to parents, who had money.'

In 1959, Cliff left home and rented a three-bedroom flat at 100 Marylebone High Street in London. It was not a dramatic departure, because he still saw his parents all the time; Tito Burns had given Rodger Webb a sinecure with a salary of £100 a week and Dorothy travelled all around the country to be with her son while he performed. However, in his own home he had a little more freedom and it was at the flat in London that he fell in love with Carol Costa.

In his short teenage life, Cliff had attracted the attention of many girls but had never seemed to care. His first steady girlfriend, Janice, had been dumped in 1958 as soon as Cliff got his first sniff of

LEFT: *Throughout Cliff's career, he sang what people wanted to hear. Each new film brought a succession of smash hits, although the critics were never very charitable about the roles he chose to play.*

LEFT: The first record to carry the billing Cliff Richard and The Shadows was 'Travellin' Light', in 1959.

fame. It was a common and not unjustified belief in the Fifties that a teen idol could not afford to have a steady girlfriend. To the fans, Cliff had to appear to be 'available'. A girlfriend would spoil his image and probably halve his record sales. Cliff Richard was not about to let that happen. 'The fans wanted to own me and I was happy with that,' he once said.

So, it was all the more unnerving for him when he found himself drawn inexorably to Carol Costa, who was living with Jet Harris in one of Cliff's spare bedrooms. He was naturally shy and sensitive around women, but with Carol he felt a strong bond, a love that he tried his best to fight. Cliff was confused about his feelings: his professional reputation was hanging in the balance and his loyalty to Jet was weighing on his mind, but all he could think about was Carol. Eventually, she decided to leave both Cliff and Jet and go home to her parents in Hounslow, London – but she would be back. While Cliff and Tony Meehan were on holiday in Italy, Carol became Mrs Jet Harris at a wedding service in Hounslow.

Meanwhile, 1959 was another very hard-working year. Cliff toured and recorded almost constantly, and 'Living Doll' was followed up by another hit –

the storming Country tune 'Travellin' Light', written by veteran New York songwriters Sid Tepper and Roy Bennett. Although Cliff did not realize it until many years later, the song had originally been written for his hero Elvis Presley for the soundtrack of the movie *King Creole*. The song was dropped from the film and Cliff made it his own, scoring a Number One hit which stayed at the top of the chart for five weeks. Once again, the B-side ('Dynamite', written by Ian Samwell) also charted, reaching Number 16. This was followed by a second studio album, *Cliff Sings*, in which he was part rock'n'roller and part balladeer, singing standards like 'Embraceable You', 'As Time Goes By' and 'The Touch Of Your Lips' with the backing of the Norrie Paramor Orchestra.

In the USA, 'Living Doll' was released on ABC Records and, although Cliff had never set foot in America, the song was a surprise hit and reached Number 30 in the chart. It was around this time that the Drifters became aware of a US vocal group of the same name who had been recording for Atlantic Records since 1953. Cliff's backing band had signed their own recording contract with Norrie Paramor in February 1959 to release

'It's not only rock'n'roll, it's hard work.'

instrumental singles and, in order to prevent any conflict, the UK Drifters decided on a change of name. They chose their new tag partly in tribute to the hip John Cassavetes movie *Shadows*, and partly because when Cliff was in the spotlight, they were usually standing behind him – in the shadows.

Cliff's first big movie, *Expresso Bongo*, was released in November. The film was a fictional biopic of a teen idol rising from a Soho coffee bar to international stardom overnight. Cliff's character was Bert Rudge, known as Bongo Herbert, a character created by screenwriter Wolf Mankowitz based on his own play, a satire of Tommy Steele (although not a million miles away from Cliff himself). The all-important soundtrack included three songs: 'Love', 'A Voice In The Wilderness' and 'The Shrine On The Second Floor', plus an instrumental called 'Bongo Blues' performed by the Shadows. In retrospect, the film was a refreshing vignette of ever-so-slightly dangerous Fifties rock'n'roll culture. It was colourful, witty and fast-moving and Laurence Harvey (who played Bongo's scheming manager Johnny Jackson) was marvellously well cast as a slippery but charismatic anti-hero.

LEFT: Tony Meehan and Jet Harris. 'Tony was a great drummer, but he wasn't pulling his weight.' – Bruce Welch

As the decade came to an end, Cliff's image took on a gloss of respectability. Gone — for the time being — was the shocking pink look, to be replaced by smart suits and soft shoes. For Christmas 1959 he proved that he was an all-round family entertainer by appearing with the Shadows in a pantomime of *Babes In The Wood* at the Globe in Stockton. Any controversy over his image dwindled away and indeed Sir Winston Churchill himself was present at the premiere of *Expresso Bongo*. When Cliff was invited to appear

'The trouble was that I never saw anyone from my record company in the whole six weeks. They should have been there. My career in America is littered with lost opportunities.'

on a variety bill in Manchester before Her Majesty the Queen Mother, his reputation got yet another boost. As his career went on, performances — and even personal audiences — before the royal family would become commonplace (he appeared at his

first Royal Variety Performance at the Victoria Palace in London before Her Majesty the Queen on May 16, 1960, in the 'youth' segment, alongside Adam Faith and Lonnie Donegan).

To capitalize on the success of 'Living Doll' Stateside, Cliff and the Shadows began their first US tour in January 1960. Billed as an 'Extra Added Attraction: England's Number One Singing Sensation', Cliff took part in a tour with Frankie Avalon and others boldly entitled the 'Biggest Show of Stars 1960', travelling across the entire North American continent. The reaction of the audience was almost as good as he might have expected back home. The crowds screamed and applauded and Cliff became

ABOVE: Yet another incarnation of the Shadows. Left to right — Brian Bennett, Hank Marvin, Bruce Welch, 'Liquorice' Locking.

RIGHT: **Expresso Bongo** *in the making. 'I found filming an incredible waste of time.' — Bruce Welch*

one of the tour's biggest attractions. 'No one could follow after we had finished,' Cliff recalls, proudly. 'The crowd were still screaming for more. It was very difficult for the next act to go on. That happened right from the first show.'

Unfortunately, America was never quite within Cliff's grasp, not least because his US record company didn't seem to know he existed. 'The trouble was that I never saw anyone from my record company in the whole six weeks,' he laments. 'They should have been there. My career in America is littered with lost opportunities.'

Even during the tour, Cliff was in such demand in Britain that as soon as the tour was over he had to fly back for the *NME* Poll-Winners' Party and for an appearance on *Sunday Night At The London Palladium* (both in one day). As the year went on, Cliff's success became almost routine and in private he was growing isolated from his friends. Unlike the Shadows, he did not smoke and had more or less given up drinking. Likewise, their careers were drifting apart as he left rock'n'roll behind in favour of more mainstream pop. The Shadows had even challenged him directly when their first hit single 'Apache' had knocked Cliff's 'Please Don't Tease' from the top of the chart in August. He seemed to have little in common with anyone he knew and only Jet's wife, Carol, seemed to understand his isolation. Her marriage was not working out well and although she and Jet now had a son, she knew that her husband had been unfaithful on a number of occasions.

Cliff bought a modest semi-detached house for himself and his parents in Percy Road, Winchmore Hill, North London, and a flashy red American Thunderbird car with a white roof. But worldly comfort was not what he needed. During the summer of 1960, he would get in his car and drive for hours, in an attempt to get away from the pressure. 'I just drive because it's rather a strain to be with people all the time,' he confided later. 'Even my mother doesn't know this. I'll just drive around for about an hour and a half and then I'll come back and I'll feel great. I go straight to sleep and wake up feeling great in the morning.'

The truth was not quite so clear cut. The relationship between Carol and Cliff had grown more serious than either of them had ever planned. One evening, Cliff told his parents that he had to spend the night in London, for business. That night he slept with Carol – the first and only sexual relationship of his life.

BELOW: Cliff's career has always been a mixture of rock'n'roller and glitzy entertainer. Here he serenades the Beverly Sisters

Unfortunately, this would not solve his personal crisis and later on he felt even more confused. He withdrew into the bosom of his family and – in a regrettably cowardly moment – asked Tony Meehan to break off the relationship on his behalf. As always, Cliff escaped the reality of his private life by throwing himself into his

---

'It's never seemed to be enough for me just to say "I've never met the right girl". Well, it just happens to be true.'

---

work. Thanks to Tito Burns, Cliff had attracted the attention of the Grade Agency, a highly influential triumvirate of three brothers: Lew Grade, proprietor of ATV; Leslie Grade, show business agent and Bernard Delfont, theatre impresario. Leslie Grade and Tito Burns struck a deal reputed to be worth £24,000 for six months' work and, in June, Cliff commenced his marathon residency at the London Palladium in a show called *Stars In Their Eyes*. The same deal would in due course lead to three films and a television show on ATV.

In October, Cliff released his third album, *Me And My Shadows*, a chummy-sounding title which rang with irony when one considered that the Shadows had been forbidden to perform 'Apache' at the Palladium shows. However, it was a mould-breaking collection because most of the songs were written by members of the Shadows, by Ian Samwell, or by their friend Pete Chester. It was completely unprecedented for a group to release an album of self-penned material (the first group to achieve this feat would be the Beatles in 1964), but Cliff made no pretence of wanting to be at the 'cutting edge' – he just wanted to record and tour, playing his own rock'n'roll.

The album, like the one before it, reached Number Two in the chart and the year ended on a high note when 'I Love You' hit the top spot on December 31. Publicly, at least, Cliff's doubts and worries seemed to have evaporated. 'I've done everything I could possibly want to do,' he said, 'and possibly everything anybody could want to do. I've got a gold disc, I've been to America, I've filmed, I've made records. So if it all ended for me, the one thing I could say is that I've lived a fuller life than most people will ever do.'

Unfortunately, just after the Christmas holiday, he received an unexpected blow. His father was taken seriously ill and rushed to hospital, where he stayed until the end of January 1961. Regrettably, when he returned from care, Rodger Webb was all the more determined to control Cliff's career and – as suddenly as he had appointed him – he sacked Tito Burns. The snubbed manager felt very hard done by, commenting later: 'I just couldn't work with [Cliff's] father. He, like a lot of others, thought he knew it all, but maybe that was because he was a very sick man.'

Three months later, on May 15, while Cliff was rehearsing for his latest movie, Rodger Webb died from a heart condition in a North London hospital. Cliff was understandably distraught and wept openly at the funeral. Rodger had become a lifeline for his son, helping Cliff to control his fears and self-doubts. Although Rodger had been sick for months, he always seemed to fight back and Cliff was very shocked at the end.

'I don't know whether he knew he was dying but he was such a stubborn man,' says Cliff, candidly. 'They actually caught him once undoing the oxygen tent so that he could have a smoke. He

managed to hide a safety pin so that he could pull the zip up from the inside. He was a dominant character right up to the end.'

Cliff's management had now been taken over by the Australian Peter Gormley, who had come to Britain while representing Frank Ifield in 1959 and started a thriving stable of artists which included the Shadows. Gormley was a character quite unlike Tito Burns. He based his relationship with Cliff purely on trust – they did not even draw up a contract. In a magnanimous gesture of good will, he waived his percentage for

ABOVE: Cliff could not get to the premiere of Summer Holiday *in London's Leicester Square because 3,000 fans barred the way.*

their first year together because he thought it unfair to take money for jobs he had not booked! By now, of course, Cliff Richard did not need a manager who could shape his career – his career was doing just fine. Gormley was to be the kind of manager who would let Cliff get on with the music without intrusion – probably the reason why their partnership was so successful and long-lasting.

The year 1960 had been incredibly prosperous, but in 1961, Cliff Richard was an even bigger hit, both at home and abroad. He toured South Africa, Scandinavia and Australasia, then came back for a six-week summer season in Blackpool. In one impressive week he had five songs in the Top Ten in India. His fourth album, *Listen To Cliff,* became the third in a row to peak at Number Two in the UK chart.

However, while Cliff did not need help with his career, his personal life was still in turmoil. In 1960, during the six-month run at the Palladium, he had started dating a 22-year-old blonde dancer called Delia Wicks. She came from Leeds and Cliff would sometimes travel north to visit her. But he thought of Delia more as a refuge from show business than a soul-mate and in 1961 he broke off the relationship after meeting another dancer, Jackie Irving, while performing in Blackpool. They were seen in public together on numerous occasions and people close to the couple thought that they might even get married, but Cliff was still unable to put his personal life before his career. He often thought about marriage, but was afraid of the commitment. He knew there was something missing, an emptiness inside, but he couldn't be sure that marriage would make a difference.

He had never taken any interest in religion and his only public comment on the subject was to note that religious beliefs 'should be private'. A year later, he would begin to realize how to fill that hollow space inside himself, by discovering his faith in Christianity.

Meanwhile, his latest movie, *The Young Ones* – his first as leading man – was widely acclaimed as one of the best British musicals of its time. With a plot unashamedly borrowed from Hollywood teen musicals like Mickey Rooney's *Babes In The Wood*, it was the story of Nicky Black (Cliff), a gutsy teenager from a wealthy background who risks his social position to save an inner-city youth club from his father's property development company. The film's producer, Kenneth Harper, gathered together a superb supporting cast in order to make Cliff look as good as possible in front of the cameras, including veteran British character actor Robert Morley, who played Cliff's father, Hamilton Black.

Tepper and Bennett (who had written Cliff's Country hit 'Travellin' Light') composed three songs for the film. The first, 'When The Girl In Your Arms Is The Girl In Your Heart', was released at the end of 1961 and went to Number

'My great ambition is to play Heathcliff in
Wuthering Heights.' — NME, 1963

Three in the chart. When the title track hit the airwaves early in 1962, it went straight into the chart at Number One, only the fourth record to do so in chart history. It stayed at the top for six weeks before being deposed by Elvis Presley's 'Rock A Hula Baby'. The song became Cliff's biggest seller so far, staying in the charts for an incredible 21 weeks. Musically, Cliff was never quite able to

break Elvis Presley's reign as the King of Rock'n'Roll – the soundtrack album of *The Young Ones* managed to knock Presley's *Blue Hawaii* off the top of the album chart for six weeks, but on the seventh week, Presley was back at Number One. However, in the cinema, Cliff was Number One by a long margin.

When *The Young Ones* was released it was a huge success and, according to the annual poll of the British film trade in *Motion Picture Herald*, Cliff Richard was the nation's most popular film star of 1962 (below him in the Top Ten box-office draws were Elvis Presley, Peter Sellers, John Wayne, Frank Sinatra and Sophia Loren, among others).

Cliff was typically modest about this success. 'For my own ego it's great to be named the top star, but my next film may be a flopperoo,' he announced, flippantly. 'I dare not compare myself with established stars like Sellers. That would be stupid . . . I know I was being used as a guinea pig to see if a British musical could be a success and I think it happened because it was a simple film with a kind of amateur charm. But the public like something simple.'

As if to verify this statement, Cliff won the 1962 Top British Singer award at the *New Musical Express* Poll-Winners' Party (for the second consecutive year) and was named Show Business Personality of the Year at the Variety Club of Great Britain annual dinner. He was also presented with a Special Award at the annual Ivor Novello Awards ceremony at London's BBC Television Centre.

That summer, Cliff was busy in Europe filming for his next film, but made another attempt to conquer the USA in September, when he returned for a short tour and appearances on *Dick Clarke's Bandstand* and the *Ed Sullivan Show*. The tour was a very clever and novel idea – a double bill consisting of a screening of *The Young Ones* (retitled for the US audience as *It's Wonderful To Be*

'THE YOUNG ONES *was just meant as a happy little film, or so we thought.*'

Young), followed by a set by Cliff Richard and the Shadows. Unfortunately, the big break just did not happen. Americans were not much interested in British singers at the best of times and this was certainly not the best of times. The tour coincided with the Cuban Missile Crisis – a time of acute political paranoia. While Cliff was trying to spread a little happiness around, many Americans were so frightened of an impending nuclear apocalypse that they didn't dare venture out of doors.

ABOVE: Cliff as a centurion in Wonderful Life. *Elstree Studios produced double sound-track LPs of* Summer Holiday *and* Wonderful Life *for the cast and crew. These are now among Cliff's most sought-after memorabilia.*

In Britain, the hits kept coming, of course. His revivals of the Peggy Lee ballad 'I'm Looking Out The Window' and the Jerry Lee Lewis rock'n'roll song 'It'll Be Me' hit Number Two in June and September 1962 respectively (both kept off the top spot by Presley). At the same time, the Shadows were Britain's most successful band. In October 1961 they had scored simultaneous Number One hits in the single, album and EP charts and 'The Savage' (an instrumental written by Norrie Paramor for *The Young Ones*) had reached Number Ten. In 1962 the hits continued with 'Guitar Tango' climbing to Number Four and their second album reaching Number One.

There can be no doubt that Cliff and the Shadows were a great team, although they were far from the fictional, fun-loving buddies that audiences were flocking to see at the cinema. Indeed, tension within the Shadows came to a head when drummer Tony Meehan and bassist Jet Harris were ejected from the band by their unofficial leader, Bruce Welch. They were replaced by Brian Bennett and Brian 'Liquorice' Locking respectively. Although he did not know it at the time, this would be a critical factor in deciding the rest of Cliff Richard's life. Locking, a top musician who had played with the Krew Kats backing Marty Wilde and Vince Taylor, was picked for his skills as a bassist, but what the Shadows did not know was that he was a devout Jehovah's Witness. It was through Cliff's conversations with 'Liquorice' that the troubled pop star finally discovered Christianity. At first, Cliff flirted with the ideas of the Jehovah's Witnesses, an interest which eventually rubbed off on his mother, but in 1962 there was not enough time to devote himself to religious study. As the year came to an end, he was back to the tour circuit promoting his latest album, *32 Minutes And 17 Seconds With Cliff Richard*. His career seemed to be taking a new twist with the release of a single which Cliff had co-written with Bruce Welch. 'Bachelor Boy', which was taken from the forthcoming film *Summer Holiday*, was a light ballad which lyrically summed up Cliff's attitude to women: 'Happy to be a bachelor boy until my dying day'. It became yet another million-seller and the movie was a blockbuster, reuniting the winning team from *The Young Ones*. This time there was a simple 'road movie'-style plot featuring Cliff and friends as London Transport engineers driving a double-decker bus across Europe to Athens. With Cliff teamed with actors Melvyn Hayes, Teddy Green and Richard O'Sullivan, the result was a bubbly cock-tail of dancing, comedy and romance. It was released just before Christmas 1962. Kenneth Harper later said that he had prayed for snow the week before the film opened. 'We were lucky; it did snow,' he remembered. 'Everybody was frozen and they went into the cinema and it was like having a summer holiday.'

In 1963, the title song of *Summer Holiday* topped the chart for two weeks and the soundtrack album remained at Number One for a stunning 14 weeks. Cliff even won another Ivor

Novello award as one of the eight writers credited for the *Summer Holiday* album, which was named as the 1963 Outstanding Score of a Musical.

At this time Cliff Richard and the Shadows were by far Britain's most popular artists, but by the end of 1963, their reign had come to a dramatic end, thanks to four floppy-fringed Liverpudlians.

ABOVE: With the Top of the Pops *dance troupe* Pan's People.

BORN AGAIN

'*All boys aren't angels, but most of them are looking for one . . .*'
— FROM RADIO LUXEMBOURG'S BOOK OF RECORD STARS, *1963*

For five years Cliff's ear for a commercial tune had been unfailing, but by 1963 he had outstayed his welcome by pop music standards. Teenagers were looking for something new, and the latest sound was the Mersey Beat.

Ironically enough, the Beatles and Cliff Richard were contemporaries who had started playing rock'n'roll music at about the same time (indeed, both John Lennon and Ringo Starr were a little older than Cliff). Of course, Cliff had been very lucky. In August 1960 while the Fab Four were unknowns, sweating their way through all-night sessions in Hamburg nightclubs, Cliff Richard was a big star back home topping the charts with 'Please Don't Tease'. Cliff and the Beatles may have started out with a mutual love of rock'n'roll, but they had taken very different routes to the top.

'There are journalists who don't like me, just because they can't put me in a bag. I refuse to be put in any musical bag.'

Cliff first sensed the end of his reign with the release of his first compilation, *Cliff's Hit Album*, which featured all of his singles from 'Move It' up to 'Do You Want To Dance?' The album was a huge success, but it peaked at Number Two in the charts, unable to dislodge the Beatles' debut *Please Please Me*. Likewise, 'She Loves You' by the Beatles had a stranglehold on the singles chart that year. It was Number One in September when Cliff's cover of the Tommy Edwards song 'It's All In The Game' stalled at Number Two and it was back at the top again in December, keeping 'Don't Talk To Him' in second place.

Cliff was still a force to be reckoned with. Indeed, his Spanish-language album *When In Spain* — which was recorded in Barcelona and intended only for export — reached Number Eight in the British chart even though most listeners could not understand a word of it. Cliff still had thousands of loyal and dedicated fans, but the majority of the screaming teens had found a new target for their adoration. In that gloomy frame of mind, Cliff and the Shadows began filming *Wonderful Life*, their least successful film. The production was doomed from the beginning. Ronald Cass and Peter Myers had written a

RIGHT: It is sometimes hard to believe the Cliff Richard of the fluffy publicity shot once played drums for The Shadows in London in 1968 when Brian Bennett was taken ill.

marvellous script set in Mexico, but Kenneth Harper announced that it would be far too expensive. The alternative was to shoot in the Canary Islands with a completely different story about a group of amateurish young film fans making a movie with equipment 'borrowed' from a pompous director (played by Walter Slezak). Despite reuniting the winning *Summer Holiday* team one more time, the formula did not work. The actors found the working conditions intolerable and the script had to be constantly rewritten in order to accommodate the changing

> *'What other people think of me is becoming less and less important. What they think of Jesus BECAUSE of me is critical.'*

weather conditions. The result was a film which was silly rather than funny and memorable only for a clever sequence in which Cliff and the cast mimic a series of legendary Hollywood stars, from the Keystone Cops to Tarzan and James Bond. 'I've always said that a musical should be fanciful,' says Ronald Cass, 'but . . . there comes a point where people reject "fanciful" and say "impossible". The screenplay grew rather than arrived.'

In a disastrous error of judgement, *Wonderful Life* was released in the same month in 1964 as the Beatles' phenomenally successful first film, *A Hard Day's Night*. There was simply no competition. This was the year of the British Invasion. The Beatles introduced Britain's pop scene to America just too late for Cliff Richard and made his successes at home seem petty and outmoded by comparison. The soundtrack to *Wonderful Life* reached Number Two in the charts behind the debut album from Britain's latest rising stars, the Rolling Stones. Compared to Mick Jagger, Cliff Richard seemed like a relic. The year came to an end with Number One hits for the Stones (the rootsy blues classic 'Little Red Rooster') and the Beatles ('I Feel Fine', their fourth consecutive million-seller). Meanwhile, Cliff was in pantomime at the London Palladium with the ageing comedian Arthur Askey. Enough said.

Thankfully, Cliff was prepared for this change in fortunes. After years of obsession with his career, his interest in Christianity had opened his eyes to a different way of life. Around this time he was introduced to a Christian evangelist who was working as a teacher at his old school in Cheshunt. An unlikely companion for a pop star, Bill Latham was a 26-year-old with no interest in rock'n'roll and with a bald pate and thick-rimmed glasses which made him look much older than his years. Despite the incongruity, Bill and Cliff became firm friends. Cliff was introduced to an interdenominational Christian youth group called Crusaders, which organized outdoor activities for teenage boys and held religious debates and Bible classes. After having learnt a lot about the

Jehovah's Witnesses, Cliff was confused but determined to get a clearer interpretation of the Bible for himself. He became a regular at the Crusaders' meetings and stimulated much debate among the members, throwing himself into religion with the same concentrated effort which he had always applied to his work. At the same time he began to see Bill Latham as a soul-mate, a friend to give him comfort and understanding who was not distracted by Cliff's fame and status. This was a refreshing time for Cliff, who had had no true friends since leaving school and had never allowed himself to make a commitment to a girlfriend. When the press first got wind of it Cliff was tentative, telling a reporter from the *Daily Express* that he had been 'thinking a lot about God'. In truth, he was letting his career slip away in favour of something far more important. He was spending all of his time with Bill Latham and the group, even forsaking his mother, who had moved to a Tudor-style mansion in Essex called Rookswood. 'Christianity

BELOW: In Take Me High, *Cliff played a merchant banker with a dream.*

> *'I can survive without stardom. I like it, but I have other things to do if it disappeared.'*

had become pre-eminent in everything I did,' he says. 'It changed my priorities. I had been rejuvenated and my career seemed uninteresting. At the same time the career of the Beatles and the Stones had shelved me and the Shadows. We were now the oldsters.'

By February 1965 he was publicly talking about his Christianity and the effects his faith had already had on his life. 'I am a Christian and I don't want anyone to get any other idea,' he told the *Melody Maker*. 'That's the way I am and I have no intention of covering up the fact.'

However, Cliff's true conversion did not happen until some time after that. His appetite for learning had been voracious, but faith cannot be forced into existence. When the moment of truth arrived, however, Cliff found faith came very easily to him. He had taken up semi-permanent residence in Bill Latham's spare bedroom in Finchley and one night – a moment he has often recounted in public – he lay in

RIGHT: Forcing smiles for the camera. As Bruce Welch said later, 'Personal feelings were getting an upper hand over our professionalism.'

his bed and opened his heart to Jesus, saying quietly to himself: 'Come on in. I want you in my life.' From that moment of spiritual certainty, Cliff was committed to Christ.

The public was scarcely aware of this change at first. Cliff's career might have taken a downturn, but he was far from absent; there was the Number One in 1965 with 'The Minute You're Gone', readers of the *New Musical Express* voted him World's Top Male Singer, he recorded three TV specials, toured Britain and Europe and appeared on the *Ed Sullivan Show* in the USA. However, on June 16, 1966, he took the biggest risk of his career and appeared at a Christian campaign rally to speak openly about his Christian faith. His manager, Peter Gormley, was very concerned that the public would be suddenly divided, perhaps thinking that this was a gimmick or dismissing Cliff as a 'wimp', but as always he left the decision to Cliff.

The rally was organized by Billy Graham, a Christian evangelist whose events attracted packed houses all around the world. In Earl's Court, London – dressed much like his friend Bill Latham in National Health specs and corduroys – Cliff appeared before 25,000 people

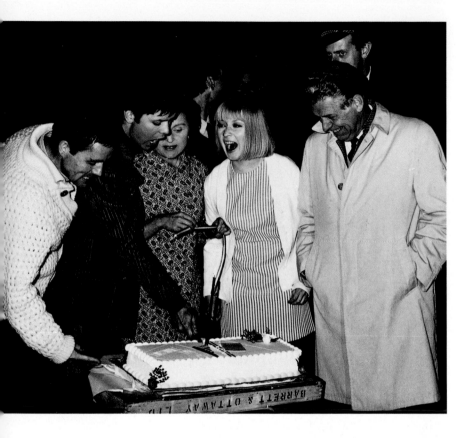

ABOVE: *Celebrations on the set of* Two A Penny. *Left to right — director James Collier, Cliff, co-stars Avril Angers and Ann Holloway, producer Frank R. Jacobson.*

'I thought Billy Graham was a charlatan until I met him.'

(while another 5,000 stood outside, listening to the rally over a special PA), proclaiming that 'until you have taken the step of asking Christ into your life, your life is not worthwhile. It works. It works for me'. He then sang a rather croaky version of the gospel song 'It Is No Secret' (which he had heard on one of Elvis Presley's gospel EPs). He

admitted later that he was more nervous than ever before in his career. In fact, when he left the podium he was completely unable to move his arms — he was literally scared stiff!

Meanwhile, Cliff's career cruised ahead blindly. There was another light-weight musical-comedy movie, *Finders Keepers*, in which Cliff and the Shadows find themselves in a deserted Spanish hotel pitching their wits against various foreign spies who are all searching for a lost secret weapon. While it wasn't an awful idea, it lacked the flair of execution which distinguished *The Young Ones* and *Summer Holiday*. Much more importantly, the film lacked good songs. Despite this set-back, Cliff's recorded output continued to be successful, including a brave attempt to put himself back into contemporary pop with 'Blue Turns To Grey' which was written by Mick Jagger and Keith Richards of the Rolling Stones.

Another major change in Cliff's life in 1966 was the marriage of his mother. Dorothy Webb's romance with her 23-year-old chauffeur had been something of a surprise to Cliff, but when they got married, he confessed to feeling somewhat relieved. 'It was the closing of one door and the opening of another,' he says. 'Up until that time I had felt responsible for my family. When my mother married, I knew I could do what I wanted – which I did. I moved in with Bill and his mother. I wanted a different scene.'

Cliff announced that in 1967 he would be taking a year off from show business.

LEFT: 'I'd rather be clean and have no hits.'

ABOVE: 'At one stage I dropped a lot of my hits from the show, but the audiences went away disappointed so I put them back in.'

With his new-found belief had come a new question weighing on his mind: was his career compatible with his faith? He was aware that many Christians viewed show business as decadent and sinful, but what else could he do? One alternative seemed to be working with children, which he had experienced both at work and with the Crusaders. He had already earned enough money to support himself for the rest of his life and so, for a while, he sat in during 'O' Level Religious Instruction classes and seriously considered retiring altogether to dedicate himself to teaching.

However his instinct to perform was always present, and he very soon realized that he could never quit. Indeed, 1967 was a busy year for him, during which he decided to marry his religious and musical interests together by recording an album of gospel songs, *Good News*, as well as songs with a religious theme for his next film project, *Two A Penny* (for which he wrote the title track himself). The film was produced by the Billy Graham movement and was a simple parable about an art student (Cliff Richard) whose discovery of Christianity leads him to question his life of delinquency and drug dealing. Again, it was not a critically or financially successful film, but at that time in his career it was certainly more valid and sincere than a silly musical set in an exotic country. For the time being, Cliff was happy to follow his instincts.

The film's story was developed with the help of David Winter, who was the editor of the Crusaders' regular newsletter. Although they often had different ideas about religion, Cliff recognized that David Winter had a great talent for transposing the morals of the church into a modern setting. Together they collaborated on two Christian books, *New Singer, New Song* and *The Way I See It*, which gave Cliff's fans an opportunity to read about and further understand his beliefs. He also appeared on a number of television and radio programmes, giving support to moral crusader Mary Whitehouse and risking ridicule by criticizing pop idols of the day for their misguided morals. He was hopelessly out of step with young people at a time when free love and experimentation with drugs were the fashion, but he stuck to his principles and fought on, proving that he was more single-minded than anyone had given him credit for. 'The public often think of him as being soft,' comments ex-Shadow Tony Meehan. 'He's a very charming and personable man but beneath that I think it's sheer metal and that doesn't come across to the public.'

In 1968 there was a brief return to former glory when Cliff Richard was chosen as Britain's entry in the annual Eurovision Song Contest, transmitted live across all the participating countries in Europe, singing 'Congratulations'. In a bizarre twist of fate, the infectiously memorable song was cheated out of first place at the eleventh hour to lose by one vote to Spain's extraordinarily banal 'La, La, La'. However, the single went on to be Number One in several countries (including the UK) and sold more than two and a quarter million copies.

After 'Congratulations', Cliff's career returned to the mundane, with a series of minor hits like 'Big Ship.' and 'With The

Eyes Of A Child', all of which failed to capture the hearts and minds of a generation in the throes of major cultural revolution. Although religion was an important issue of the day (particularly in Northern Ireland), Cliff's cheerful optimism seemed totally divorced from the world's obsession with LBJ, Vietnam, mass communications and the space race. Meanwhile, the Shadows were also finding it impossible to maintain their place in the charts and at the end of 1968 they split up, re-forming temporarily in 1969 to tour Britain and Japan with Cliff (but without Bruce Welch). Without the Shadows behind him Cliff was considerably hindered, though he was successful at first, launching a full-scale European tour with folk-rockers the Settlers. Cliff and his new backing band played a three-part gospel show called *Help, Hope and Hallelujah*, combining hymns, gospel songs and secular numbers with a moral message.

For other concerts, he would be backed by a selection of session musicians who wore black against a black backcloth, keeping him constantly in the spotlight. Where once he had been the frontman for a popular and inventive group, he was now a frumpy celebrity. As if to confirm

RIGHT: 'Television still frightens me a little . . . I always have the feeling of all those unseen viewers.'

this, his TV career, which began in earnest in the early Seventies, consisted of insipid variety shows featuring lightweight comedy sketches, songs and celebrity guests that made predictable viewing, although he did earn an award from Mary Whitehouse's National Viewers' and Listeners' Association.

To expand his experience as an actor, he took a role in a production of Peter Shaffer's *Five Finger Exercise* at the New Theatre, Bromley, in Kent. It was a story about a young man investigating his sexual identity, rather incompatible with his own beliefs. Cliff was successful enough to be invited back a year later to appear in Graham Greene's *The Potting Shed* (which was hurriedly transferred to the Sadler's Wells in London when the New Theatre burned down two days before opening night).

In 1972 he appeared in the television production *The Case*, a musical comedy-thriller co-starring Tim Brooke-Taylor and singer Olivia Newton-John (Bruce Welch's girlfriend), and returned to the big screen for the last time in *Take Me High*, with Debbie Watling and George Cole. Produced by Kenneth Harper once again, the film had a score of Cliff Richard tracks, but no song and dance

set-pieces. The paper-thin story about a merchant banker going to Birmingham to run a burger restaurant was a non-starter and the film flopped at the box office, failing to recoup its costs.

Cliff's other main interest outside music was charity work, and it was

ABOVE: Tennis became a new passion in the 1980s.

his commitment to needy causes which finally helped him to turn his career around. His friend Bill Latham gave up his job teaching in Cheshunt to run a new Christian charity called The Evangelical Alliance Relief Fund, or TEAR Fund for short. In November 1973 Cliff flew to

---

'The fact is, I'm not whiter than white — at the best I'm rather a dirty grey.'

Bangladesh, which was overflowing with refugees from neighbouring India. TEAR was helping to supply the refugees with food, medicine and other essentials, but when Cliff arrived he found the camps in a distressing state. As he was given a tour of one camp, he witnessed people dying of malnutrition all around him. As he held a small boy in his arms and the desperate child clung to him for dear life, Cliff was horrified. Immediately, he offered to stay and help, but the aid workers shocked him with their reply — they told him to go home. They needed nurses, not pop singers. If Cliff wanted to help he should go back to London and tell everyone what he had seen. He did just that, and his work on behalf of the world's poor and needy has been the driving force of his career ever since. Rationalizing that God had given him the gift of song for a good reason, he became more determined than ever to put his voice to good use. Since then, in addition to his many benefit concerts, Cliff has donated at least ten per cent of all his earnings to charities. 'I've been praying for a long time that God would help me use my money correctly,' he said in 1974. 'Maybe it will come to a point where I'll just sign away everything as I earn it. I'm quite prepared to do that if God tells me.'

In 1975, for the first time since his career began, Cliff failed to have a chart hit. He might have scored a chart success with the catchy '(There's A) Honky Tonk Angel (Who Will Take Me Back In)', but when Cliff was informed that 'honky tonk angel' was American slang for a prostitute, he withdrew the record immediately. One way or another he seemed fated to be kept out of the singles chart for the time being. 'He was making boring, bland records and he didn't seem to care,' commented Bruce Welch. 'The only thing in his life was religion.'

Cliff had tried his hand at writing his own songs and even composed half of the material on his 1974 LP, *31st Of February Street*, which was a personal — if not commercial — success. However, in September 1975 he went into Abbey Road studios with Bruce Welch as his producer and recorded some songs for his next album. It would prove to be his most challenging and successful studio session in years. The first song, 'Miss You Nights', put Cliff back in the Top Twenty for the first time in two years in February 1976. The second, 'Devil Woman', was a totally new sound for Cliff and reached Number Nine.

It was not his most successful British record by a long way, but in the USA 'Devil Woman' was his all-time biggest hit, reaching Number Six in the charts. Moreover, this song reminded the public — and Cliff himself — that he was still capable of pulling a surprise.

By contrast to his recent output, 'Devil Woman' was dark and sinister-sounding. It hinted at a sensuality long absent from Cliff's repertoire. 'I knew what I was capable of, but I'd happily got into doing family shows,' Cliff said. 'It was the first time in years that I'd had the chance to stretch my voice and do some

rock.' The resulting album, *I'm Nearly Famous*, was described by commentators as 'the renaissance of Cliff Richard', and it was his first Top Five LP since *Wonderful Life* (apart from the compilation *The Best Of Cliff* in 1969). Although the full revival of his reputation was still not assured, Cliff was getting ready to groove once more.

ABOVE: Cliff duetting with Phil Everly on 'She Means Nothing To Me', a UK Top Ten hit in 1983.

ARISE SIR CLIFF

'The one thing youth has is energy,
but what it doesn't have, and can never
have, is wisdom. You have to get older to
have wisdom.'

After the critical and financial success of *I'm Nearly Famous*, Cliff invited Bruce Welch to stay on as his producer, but somehow the magic of those early sessions was gone. The partnership nearly ended with the two lowest chart positions in Cliff's singing career, Number 46 for 'When Two Worlds Drift Apart' and Number 57 for 'Green Light'. In 1977 he produced an album of gospel material himself called *Small Corners* and then, in 1979, he suddenly realized that he had a couple of aces up his sleeve. Alan Tarney and Terry Britten, session musicians who had been working with him since the early Seventies, had developed a strong partnership. Together they would recharge Cliff's batteries and give a chart-busting contemporary edge to his work.

After his sold-out 24-night 20th Anniversary tour ended in December 1978, Cliff and Britten collaborated on the recording of his next album, *Rock And Roll Juvenile*, at Pathé Marconi Studios in Paris. The majority of the songs were written by Tony Britten with the lyricist B. A. Robertson (who went on to have a solo hit with 'Bang Bang' in 1979). Apart from a contribution at the beginning as producer, Bruce Welch did not participate in the recording of the album.

The following year began with a good omen – in the Queen's New Year's Honours list Cliff was awarded an OBE (Order of the British Empire), which was presented by the Queen at Buckingham Palace in July. Then, in August, Cliff scored his first Number One hit since

---

'I'm very fond of her and I guess it's because we never got involved that we can remain such good friends. When we see each other we hug each other to death for about ten minutes.'

CLIFF ON OLIVIA NEWTON-JOHN

1968 with 'We Don't Talk Any More', written by Tarney. Ironically, this was the only track on the album which had been produced by Bruce Welch. The song even went Top Ten in the USA and eventually sold just under three million copies worldwide! *Rock And Roll Juvenile* reached Number Three and stayed in the charts for 22 weeks – longer than any album since *Summer Holiday*. Cliff Richard was a

LEFT: *In 1961, Cliff was asked what he would be doing at the age of 50. 'Sweeping the streets I should imagine,' he replied.*

superstar once again, and nothing could stop him.

Alan Tarney produced the next album, *I'm No Hero*, which reached Number Four on its release in 1980. Cliff was now a regular in the singles charts on both sides of the Atlantic. The bluesy 'Carrie' reached Number Four in the UK and Number 34 in the USA; 'Dreamin' (co-written by Tarney and Leo Sayer) reached Number Eight in the UK and Number Ten in the USA; and 'Suddenly' (a duet

ABOVE: Olivia Newton-John, who lived with Bruce Welch from 1966 to 1972.

> *'I want to be married. I love kids and would like to have some of my own. And my mother is a bit anxious. She keeps introducing me to nice, single girls in that special way that mothers do. But nothing has happened yet.'*
> CLIFF IN 1976

with Olivia Newton-John lifted from her movie *Xanadu*) got to Number 15 in the UK and Number 20 in the USA.

During March and April 1981 Cliff spent seven weeks touring the US and Canada, playing a set which was almost exclusively recent material (it must have been a refreshing change to go out on stage and not have to sing 'Living Doll').

He then returned to the studio with Alan Tarney to record *Wired For Sound*. Once again, the album had a very contemporary sound (B. A. Robertson's lyric for the title track — as illustrated in the video promo — was a paean to the current craze for personal stereos!) and sold in excess of a million copies. That was followed up in December with another smash single, a live version of Shep & The Limelites 'Daddy's Home', which rocketed to Number Two (it made Number 23 in the USA in March 1982).

In 1982 Cliff toured the world, playing in Hong Kong, Singapore, Bangkok, Australia, New Zealand, Kenya, Europe and the USA, spent a week in Kenya on behalf of the TEAR Fund and released another gospel album, *Now You See Me . . . Now You Don't*. Despite all that hard work, the year was most notable for a new twist in his personal life. For the first time since his relationship with Jackie Irving in the 1960s, Cliff admitted to being romantically linked to a woman. In the 1970s the press had tried to contrive a relationship between Cliff and Olivia Newton-John, despite their constant claims that they were just good friends. However, when Cliff flew to Denmark to watch British tennis star Sue Barker play an exhibition match, the newspapers

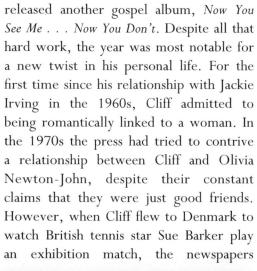

BELOW: Alan Tarney (left) produced I'm No Hero *and* Wired For Sound *and played bass in Cliff's band.*

immediately announced that a marriage was in the offing. During the Wimbledon tournament that summer, they were seen kissing publicly and Cliff even flippantly suggested to journalists that they were 'the new Charles and Di' (meaning that they were having a fairy-tale romance, not a bitter separation!). Like Cliff, the 25-year-old sportswoman had braved the ridicule of the press to announce her new-found Christianity and the couple had been drawn together by their similar experiences. During that summer they became virtually inseparable. At the same time, Bill Latham was seeing an English girl whom he had met in South Africa while touring with Cliff, and the two couples were regularly seen on double dates together. However, in August Cliff went on holiday to Bermuda with his mother (whose marriage had recently ended) and friends from the Crusaders. During that time, the pressure of speculation built up in the newspapers back home, challenging Cliff and Sue to get married. When Cliff got back, Sue had to go away for a tournament and by the time they were finally reunited, the spark of romance between them had gone. 'I think that during the summer we had probably seen too much of each other,' says Sue. 'It may not have

LEFT: 'I don't think Cliff Richard could act his way into a deserted railway station.' — theatre critic John Peters reviews Time *in the* Sunday Times.

been good career-wise, but we were having fun.'

Cliff later said that he had considered proposing to Sue, but never felt that marriage would be suited to him and the relationship fizzled out, even though they carried on meeting up as friends. He candidly admitted that his freedom and his career were the most important things in his life: 'The love that I have for Sue was overshadowed by the fact that I love my lifestyle that much more'.

After the romance had died down, the press had another cause to get overexcited when Cliff celebrated his 25th Anniversary in 1983, culminating in the Silver Tour, featuring six weeks of sold-out concerts at the Apollo Victoria Theatre in London.

After *Wired For Sound* his chart record took a slight dip, but the regular touring continued until the end of 1985, when he became committed to starring in a West End theatre production. Produced by Dave Clarke, the play was a science-fiction musical called *Time*, a morality tale about a pop star trying to convince a mighty Time Lord that the Earth should be saved from apocalypse. The musical encouraged all people to be tolerant and kind to one another, although it did not synchronize with Cliff's beliefs because it was not completely based around a religious concept. Nevertheless, Cliff threw himself wholeheartedly into the project and the first fruits of his labours appeared in September 1985 with a single produced and arranged by Stevie Wonder featuring Cliff on vocals called 'She's So

---

'I've always considered myself a hairy rocker.'

Beautiful', which charted at Number 17.

However, before the musical opened, Cliff scored a massive, unexpected Number One hit with a golden oldie – a novelty version of 'The Young Ones' featuring silly voices from the fashionable alternative comedians of the same name. The single was hastily recorded with Hank Marvin guesting on guitar in support of the charity Comic Relief and topped the charts for three weeks, selling more than half a million copies.

Time received terrible reviews and was even described as 'one of the century's worst musicals', but it proved to be very popular. This may have been due to the sophisticated special effects used in the production, which included a three-dimensional, animated hologram of Sir Laurence Olivier, but was probably because the appeal of Cliff Richard himself was incredibly potent. The soundtrack album — which featured a host of stars including Freddie Mercury, Dionne Warwick and Julian Lennon — rose to Number 21 in the chart. Meanwhile, Cliff had an even bigger hit with a song from the rival musical *Phantom of the Opera* by Andrew Lloyd-Webber. The song was called 'All I Ask Of You' and eventually

BELOW: Sue Barker retired from professional tennis in the mid-1980s and married in 1988. She is now a sports commentator.

gave Cliff a Number Three hit.

Cliff's theatre project was an unqualified success at the box office. He gave eight sold-out performances of *Time* every week for a full 12 months, selling over 700,000 tickets before he bowed out

'Am I sticking up two fingers to my critics by having a big concert at Wembley? Not as much as two fingers, no. Maybe one finger. No, one finger's worse than two, isn't it?'

on April 11, 1987. (He was replaced by David Cassidy, but the production closed six months later.)

Boosted by this triumph, he reunited with Alan Tarney, determined to release another bestselling pop LP. So, while still appearing in *Time*, Cliff worked tirelessly to produce *Always Guaranteed*, one of his best and most successful albums ever, which eventually sold one and a third million copies (in Denmark it was awarded a platinum disc — only the second album ever to receive the award in Danish pop music history!). Tarney played virtually all instruments on the album – guitar, bass, keyboards and drum machines – and gave the record a sound which was totally up-to-the-minute. 'He really wants to remain a contemporary artist,' commented Alan Tarney. 'If Jason Donovan is the latest heart throb then Cliff would like nothing better than to get up there and show him how it should be done. That's what keeps him going.'

To prove it, Cliff released four singles from the new album, two of which ('Some People' and 'My Pretty One') went Top Ten. Since then, he has almost never slipped from the public eye, with a touring and recording schedule which would cause most men half his age to wither from exhaustion. To support the album he set off on his most ambitious touring spectacular yet. Three warm-up shows at the Wimbledon Theatre were followed by a 50-date European tour culminating with six nights at the National Exhibition Centre (NEC) in Birmingham. The following year, in commemoration of the thirtieth anniversary of his first hit, he toured Australia, New Zealand and Europe before embarking on a mammoth UK tour. Yet again he broke his own records by selling out all 47 venues within 72 hours. Cliff played to more than 200,000 people and ended the

year with his ninety-ninth single, 'Mistletoe And Wine'. It was another massive hit and quickly became the best-selling single of the year, shifting more than 750,000 units by the end of 1988. His thirtieth anniversary year ended with Cliff not only at Number One in the

ABOVE: In 1993, Cliff joined his old sparring partner to sing a new version of 'Move It' on Hank Plays Cliff.

singles charts, but also Number One in the album and video charts with his double album compilation *Private Collection*.

It seemed that nothing could outdo these successes, yet in 1989 he was determined to do just that. His one hundredth hit single, 'The Best Of Me', was a slight

BELOW: In the 1990s, Cliff is as popular as ever.

disappointment, but the advance publicity was sufficient for it to enter the charts at Number Two in the first week of release. A week later he was in London for the biggest shows of his entire career: 'Cliff Richard – The Event' consisted of two sold-out appearances at the massive Wembley Stadium, each to a crowd of 72,000 people. In July he was out on the road for a series of low-key gospel shows and in August he was once again back on daytime radio with the exceptionally catchy 'I Just Don't Have The Heart'. Written by the winning team of Stock, Aitken and Waterman (the masterminds behind the pop stardom of Kylie Minogue and Jason Donovan, amongst others), it reached Number Three in the charts and proved once more that Cliff's appeal was as broad as ever.

Taking 'The Event' as a template, Cliff went back on the road in 1990 with a show in two halves, an *Oh Boy!* collection full of rock'n'roll oldies followed by a second half of recent hits. Again, the gigs were a huge success. Cliff celebrated his fiftieth birthday by selling out 14 nights at the NEC in Birmingham and 18 nights at the Wembley Arena and once again having a Number One hit at Christmas with the festive song 'Saviour's Day'.

Always continuing his charitable work, he began 1991 with a 12-date gospel tour ending at the Royal Albert Hall in London on Easter Saturday and he added yet another string to his bow in 1992 with the launch of the Cliff Richard Tennis Trail, a scheme to encourage young children in UK primary schools to take up tennis and perhaps become the Wimbledon stars of the future. In the meantime, he recorded a Top Ten album, *Together*, filmed two Christmas specials for TV and spent a week in Uganda making a film for the TEAR Fund.

Once again in 1992 he was back on stage, this time with the thrilling Access All Areas Tour, including 13 dates at the NEC in Birmingham, five at Sheffield Arena, three at Glasgow's SECC and finally 16 at Wembley Arena, becoming Britain's biggest live draw of the year with a total audience of more than 420,000 fans. But Cliff was still full of energy. The following Easter he was back with another gospel tour, raising £100,000 for charity, and in May there was *Cliff Richard – The Album*, another brilliantly chosen collection of contemporary material by writers like Nik Kershaw and Pete Sinfield, which entered the chart at Number One. Meanwhile,

> *'When I was 18, people of 40 hated rock. Now, when we're 60 . . . it may sound ridiculous, but I'm going to love rock; the music will still be OUR music.'*

Cliff was embarking on a highly successful tour of Europe and the United Arab Emirates.

The year of 1994 was devoted to making arrangements for a return to the West End stage with Cliff's latest pet project, a musical version of the famous nineteenth-century novel *Wuthering Heights* by Emily Brontë. The production was to be based around five songs, composed by John Farrar and noted lyricist Sir Tim Rice. However, once the first five songs were recorded and the play began to take shape, it became clear that it was going to be on a very grand scale. Cliff had hoped to schedule the opening night for November 1994, but this was no longer feasible. So, instead of a musical, Cliff decided to embark on yet another massive pop tour. His thirty-fifth anniversary in showbiz neatly coincided with 30 Top Five singles, which were collected (along with his personal choice, 'Green Light') on the *Hit List* album. Similarly, the tour served as a showcase for Cliff's old favourites on a colourful stage shaped like a giant jukebox. He packed out 31 dates from Birmingham to Dublin, continuing in 1995 to the Far East, New Zealand, Australia and South Africa (his first

---

'I've never really worried about making money — I don't to this day know how much I earn.'

---

concerts there in almost 20 years, before audiences of up to 30,000 people!).

The *Heathcliff* album finally took shape in Los Angeles, where he recorded three songs with Olivia Newton-John in 1995. The album was his most sumptuous and adventurous in years and Cliff immersed himself in the characters with typical dedication. In the story, Heathcliff is denounced and deceived by his lover, Cathy, who marries another man. Heathcliff then goes abroad to seek his

fortune and returns to take his revenge, finally driving Cathy into madness and death. Cliff performed the title role on stage, of course, but on the album he performed all male voices, and Olivia Newton-John took the role of Cathy. The show itself opened with the first single, 'Misunderstood Man' (as sung by a narrator, rather than Heathcliff himself), which asks the audience to decide whether Heathcliff is truly despicable or just misunderstood. This is the great dilemma which makes *Heathcliff* such a tragic story – why do these lovers destroy each other? Beginning and ending with Heathcliff at Cathy's graveside, the musical is an emotional rollercoaster and Cliff considers the music to be 'the best and most important album of my career.' At the time of writing, the production is scheduled for a three-week preview in Birmingham before moving on to the West End in November 1996.

Arguably the most important moment in Cliff's recent career took place in 1995. He was deeply honoured to be invited to appear as one of the artists at the VE Day celebrations both in Hyde Park and in front of Buckingham Palace. Yet nothing could compare to the feeling when, a few weeks later, it was

announced that he had been awarded a knighthood in the Queen's Birthday Honours List for his services to charity. Not only was this a recognition of Cliff's work, but also a vindication of his efforts to unite his love of rock'n'roll and his strict Christian principles.

In the mid-1970s, when he had considered leaving show business, Cliff Richard had asked himself whether it was possible to bring together his work as a pop star and as a Christian. We can only be thankful that he made the right decision. In the last 20 years, Cliff has brought many hours of happiness to his fans while maintaining his commitment to the poor and needy. No other singer, not even the esteemed Bob Geldof, has done so much to help others while remaining so consistently popular. Though the critics may chide him for his celibacy and his Peter Pan looks, he can always turn to his CD and ticket sales to remember that critics do not pay the bills. Cynical journalists and music pundits are quick to scoff, but with every few years comes a new generation of Cliff Richard fans. Reading his press cuttings only goes to prove that nobody likes Cliff Richard, except the public.

LEFT: Songs from Heathcliff were showcased in a 25-minute performance at the Royal Variety Show in November 1995.